I0161476

Kuji-in Mastery

Power of Manifestation

by MahaVajra

F.Lepine Publishing

http://www.kujiin.com

© François Lépine 2008

ISBN: 978-1-926659-27-5

Table of contents

The Source of Wisdom and Power

The Nine Hand Seal techniques did not generate the wisdom that come from their application, but it is in fact the other way around. The ancient wisdom of the Hindu and Buddhist people who assembled Kuji-In over the millenniums, was contemplated, and it eventually lead to the resulting ritual practice that resumes this wisdom, giving birth to the technique we now know as Kuji-In. Thereafter, the application of the technique contributes to the reintegration of the sacred knowledge that first helped in creating it, making its way into the consciousness of the student who practices the ritual technique.

Afterwards, the delicate origin of this system of knowledge that composes Kuji-In was lost, and for many users, only the ritual practice remained. Yet, the simple application of the ritual technique will not suffice in restoring the beauty and power it was intended for in the first place. The efficiency of the mudras will work wonders by themselves, in time. So will the mantras and the mental imagery. Yet, the Nine Hand Seals complete system was not intended to take effect "in time", but quickly and efficiently. While the physical and mental aspects of the technique are easy to remember and apply, the true secret lies in the contemplation of the wisdom that is also an important part of the entire process.

By applying the ritual practice while also seeking the knowledge that once lead to it, the Kuji-In process becomes complete and it produces the most powerful and efficient expansion of the consciousness, which is the goal of its practice. The physical and mental components are used to tune the mind and the body into the spiritual process. Without a physical element, the effect would not manifest as quickly. Without a mental element, the effect would not interact with our conscious perception with such efficiency.

Every aspect of this technique was carefully crafted in ways to develop the whole of the being at each of the different levels it addresses itself to our conscious experience of life. Each of the nine steps of the Kuji-In process takes care of an entire area of our existence. For each step, the mudra was carefully selected, the mantra was thoroughly pondered, the mental imagery styles and attitudes were crafted with care, all in ways to reflect the original wisdom it was intended to awaken in the new student.

Changing one's life is often challenged with hesitation, doubt and fear of the unknown. It is a constant path to travel as your thrive to learn more, acquiring new knowledge everyday, yet keeping an attitude of innocence, paying attention to every new reaction that arise in you, being humble enough to acknowledge they are yours.

In order to develop your self, it will not suffice simply to apply the adequate ritual technique of the Kuji-In. With lots of practice you will notice your attitude changes, but by willingly changing your attitude, you will se your entire existence change.

Kuji-In was built with the sole purpose of quickly transforming our lives for the better, to enhance our abilities in whatever we do, and open our horizons to experiences we did not dare to dream of. Be respectful of the technique as it is thought to you, and set your mind in a sacred state for each practice; the results will be efficient at first, profound as you go on, and extraordinary in due time.

The sacred state of mind

The goal of self development and transformation is to find your Spirit inside you, and not necessarily to pray an outside God. In fact, it is not a necessity for you to define God at all. You can practice Kuji-In and adapt the spirituality of the teachings to your own definition of an absolute force of the universe, whatever you selected. Your Spirit is your own self-Divinity, your first envelope over the absolute truth of the all-encompassing source of creation, regardless of the name you choose to define this source.

By getting into yourself, even doing your own little thing, is in fact getting in touch with highest of you, from the inside, which is perfect. The sacred attitude is very different than to have a dogma to believe in. Simply by doing a little prayer, even to your own Spirit, without naming any God of invoking any name, you are in fact getting into a sacred attitude. The simple fact of taking a few seconds to say aloud that you are setting yourself in a sacred attitude, and doing Kuji-In for the development of yourself in Spirit, is setting your mind into a sacred attitude.

It would be arrogant if you said to yourself that you don't need to do any kind of prayer or spiritual affirmation, that Kuji-In is to make you powerful without the help of your Spirit. That thought is simply idiot, and a contradiction in itself. Right now, you are getting in touch with what you really are inside, and this is perfect. The belief in an outside God is not a requirement at all. An outside God is for religion. Kuji-In is not about religion, it is about yourself. Know that Kuji-In is useless without the interaction with your Spirit. Take the time to say physically that you are entering a privilege time for yourself, and invoke the presence of your Spirit within, and you will be on the good path. I'd even say this is the goal of Kuji-In mastery, which is to call within the power of your Spirit so it can project itself outwardly in your physical experience, thus manifesting supernatural events and developing new perceptive abilities.

For example, you could say to yourself:

"I hereby enter into a sacred state of mind, to have a privilege relationship with my Spirit." Then take a deep breathe, and pay attention to how you feel, even if you don't feel anything in particular. Paying attention will provoke the communion, even a silent gentle one.

That little statement would be enough to set your mind in a sacred attitude. Then, those who wish to combine their personal spiritual experience with their relationship with the God of their belief are welcome to do so.

The main reason why some people pursue a spiritual path in a religion or with a spiritual master is that they are steadily encouraged to go further, to go beyond your limits, where otherwise they might have chosen to remain bounded by their own judgments and fears, hindering their progress. To face yourself as you are in truth, it either takes some outside encouragement, or plain courage.

The Spirit

The perseverant application of the Kuji-In technique will progressively rebuild the bond you have with your own Spirit. It clears a path for yourself as a Spirit, to enter and flow thru yourself as a human. By paying attention to the silent presence inside you, you will eventually feel someone is there, someone you know is you, but it is not the person you know yourself to be. It is not a human identity, or a person, like the one you are used to be in contact with. It is of a higher nature, completely silent, and holy present, like if you were looking at yourself from within.

Through our human life experience, we conditioned ourselves with beliefs, and we adopted a set of definitions that we could relate to in order to identify ourselves as who we are. We build our own human identity. The Spirit has nothing to do with conditioning and identification. It is void of any definition, free from intellectual limitations, since it exists way beyond our human mind. It thinks and lives in ways that we are not yet aware of, as human. For the human being, the Spirit is felt as a presence, like an exterior force, but felt inside.

This presence is not you, as a human, with personality traits, a character and an identity. It is you as Spirit. At first, it might even seem to be someone else, and this feeling would be appropriate, since your human self perceives this new presence as someone else. Of course, it is not your human identity, and it is normal that this new presence is felt as an "other".

From a human point of view, the Spirit seems to be separate, alien to the human personal definition we built for ourselves. Gradually, while allowing yourself to feel this new presence, which is you at another level of consciousness, you become acquainted to feeling one with your Spirit, and your human self will allow this new presence to enter into its definition of self. This is the process thru which the human self gradually accepts the presence of the Spirit self, to join with your human identity. In time, this joining will become a remembering of who you are, from a higher point of view, and the separation between your human and spiritual self will vanish into consciousness.

The key is simple, pay attention. After every practice, meditation and relaxation, listen, look, smell, taste and feel within. Try to find this presence or let it reveal itself to you. Allow it be present.

Contemplative Technique

We previously learned how to actively implicate ourselves in the ritual application of Kuji-in. The reason for this was to stimulate our ability to project willpower thru the technique. Also, it is easier to concentrate on all aspects of a Kuji-In set while we are completely awake and mentally active. Now that we advanced in the learning process, we will change our approach.

The Kuji-In techniques as they will be shown to you here should be practiced in the contemplative manner. By contemplative, we mean that you should mentally gaze at the visualization, ponder the philosophical concept, and gently hold the mudra in a comfortable position, so that your mind can slowly go into a meditative state. After going thru all the details of a technique, we wish to find a mental state between conscious application of the technique, and transcendence. Not to transcend up to a point where we would lose consciousness, but not be so humanly present as to prevent any interaction with our Spirit.

For each set, take to time to ponder each of the concepts profoundly. Study the links between the different aspects of each technique. The more globally you will learn about each trait of

Kuji-In, the more your mind and brain will reserve some space in them for Kuji-In to take place. You might even re-read the philosophy suggested in the Advanced Kuji-In book, to make as much links as possible.

Once you understand the general intellectual envelope of a Kuji-In set, set yourself in a relaxed position, and wander off into the realms of consciousness that Kuji-In will awaken in you. Apply the technique in gentle contemplation, while keeping in mind as much as you can, without effort. In each of your practice periods, your mind will select specific aspects of the technique to gaze upon.

Let this be an exploration for your consciousness, while holding on the base of the ritual technique. We do not recommend going into a complete state of letting go, or it would not be Kuji-In anymore, but another experience baring other names. At this point we want to use the experience you have built with your prior Kuji-In practice to actively affirm a link with your Spirit, while also remaining passively sensible enough to perceive what your Spirit could reveal to you. Your human ego might play tricks on you. Use your discernment and stay focused on Kuji-In as you learned it, without judging what could be a genuine revelation of your Spirit. Your Spirit will not change the Kuji-In technique since it doesn't care about the technique. It will reveal to you who you are.

Breathe and Consciousness

Prana, the energy that flows in the air and in all of nature, is mostly available to the human thru breathe. Breathe allows our body to assimilate oxygen, and on the energy level, our energy body assimilates prana, the life giving energy available everywhere.

Each Kuji-In set should be done in a comfortable physical posture, allowing your breathe to flow freely, and in a relaxed state of mind, allowing your energy system to assimilate as much prana as possible. Do not force this process with hard concentration. Allow it to take place, with a relaxed mental focus.

Start your Kuji-In practice period with a bit of free conscious breathing, or a breathing technique you appreciate. Be aware of the physical air flowing thru your nasal cavities, and pay attention to the energy that enters your energy system at the bridge of your eyebrows and the top of the nose. This energy naturally flows up your cranial bone in the center of your head, to the back of your skull, and down your spine.

The more you pay attention to the flow of prana when it enters your body, the more you bathe your brain cells in this activating energy, producing changes in your mind and in your physical brain. But mostly, while you pay attention, you allow yourself to become aware of other aspects of your Spirit and its possible manifestation in your physical existence.

Thru your breath, consciousness travels. Breathe gives life, and Spirit can flow thru life. Start every practice with this breathing affirmation of consciousness. It will allow your Spirit to flow thru your human self with ease, and progressively, you will remember who you are.

From now on, each time you finish a chapter, and each time you go thru an aspect of the knowledge that moves you, take a deep relaxed breathe, and pay attention. Let the knowledge integrate your mind. Let the energy integrate your body. Let the Spirit reveal itself to you.

The Human Ego

The human ego is composed of all that we have defined for ourselves as being the reality we live in. It is a set of interpretations of our human experiences that does all it can to pull itself into a single cognitive entity, that we call by our personal name. The human ego has no idea of what Spirit is. Before you have been often enough in contact with yourself as Spirit, your human ego will be afraid of this contact, because we fear what we do not know, and our human ego only knows itself.

Our human ego has some consciousness of itself, and it takes decisions in function of retaining as much of our attention as possible. The more it can use our human existence, the happier it is. This is why we must not take our ego as an enemy, but we should do all we can to consider it a friend. By working to erase our human ego, we are trying to destroy what presently help us define our existence. By befriending our human ego, we are appropriate ourselves a wonderful tool to work with while we still need its definitions to function as human beings.

In time, by elevating ourselves and rebuilding our personal definitions at a higher level of consciousness, we will encourage the interaction of our Spirit with our human identity. The presence of our Spirit in our human consciousness will slowly transmute our human ego into a better tool to serve our spiritual objectives. Until then, we have to trust ourselves and work with our human ego, since it is the most powerful tool we have at the moment.

Our human ego is the tools we possess, that cannot be taken away. If we take the time to learn about ourselves and understand our ego, we will become aware of its inner workings and it will become much easier to transform ourselves for the better, until the Spiritual transmutation can occur.

At first, our ego will fight to prevent repeated interactions with our Sprit. Our ego feels the transmuting effect of the Spirit, and it is afraid that by accepting the Spirit, it will lose itself and be destroyed. In fact, the Spirit does not destroy the ego when it transmutes it, but preserves it in a higher state of existence.

Take the time to adopt yourself as a human ego as well as yourself as Spirit. Both are the same, both are one, only the ego perceives all of the spiritual realms from below, shaded by the illusionary rifts of humanness, and the Spirit perceives from everywhere, seeing only perfection at work.

Binding Hands and Fingers

The hands themselves hold many mysteries, and we will unfold but a few in the following chapters. Each hand can hold many representations, and some of those representations have been classified thru the ages, in a simple set of correspondence with other aspects of our human and spiritual nature. Since many variations exist to kuji-in, keep in mind that this system of classification is from the Transformational Approach, and that other systems as wise and legitimate, each for their own purpose.

The left hand usually represents the feminine, receptive, taking, passive hand, while the right hand would represent the masculine, emitting, giving, active hand. In our quest to understand the wisdom implicated in the practice of Kuji-In, we will tend to define the left hand as the human hand, and the right hand as the spiritual hand.

Like in any system of analogical classification, the relations we make are close to metaphors than to the physical truth. Let us keep in mind that the right hand can receive, and the left hand can give, even if the usual charts of correspondences would state otherwise.

In the same way, the left hand is as spiritual as the right, and the right hand as human as the left.

Nevertheless, let us imagine for a moment that the ritual gestures we do in Kuji-In with our left hand would be the representation of our human implication in the technique, and that our right hand would represent the implication of the Spirit. It would be reasonable to state, in most sets of the technique, that both human and Spirit are working together harmoniously, since most of the mudras hold a good symmetry. But it is not the fact for the mudra of Retsu and Zen, the 7th and 9th set, where the mudras are asymmetric. Still, they are harmonious in their workings and we will explain the details of this in due time.

As for the hands, each of the fingers represents an aspect of our human and spiritual nature. When we bind our hands and fingers together, not only do we use the beneficial combinations of different energy meridians, but we also affirm a conceptual representation of these aspects of nature working together to attain the desired goal. In the same ways that the drawing of a symbol may awaken some vibration pattern corresponding to its signification, the placement of our fingers in a set of symbolic gestures may awaken these energy patterns on the energy and spiritual planes of existence.

There are already many sets of symbolic classifications of the fingers, and one of those sets exists for Kuji-In. For each set of the Kuji-In, we will resume the different traits that we find pertinent to the application of our techniques, and we will explain the symbolic representation of the finger placement for each mudra.

Let us resume the signification of each finger, alone.

The thumb is the finger representing the contemplative, observing nature of consciousness. It is associated with the element "void", the fifth element. It is awareness, in the form of a presence. In the left hand, it represents the human aware of itself. In the right hand, it represents the awareness of the Spirit as well as the presence of the Spirit.

The index is the finger representing the concept of affirmation. It is the pointing finger, expressing itself, confirming its power. It is associated with the element of air, flowing forward swiftly. In the left hand, it is the typical affirmation of our human will. In the right hand, it is the implication of our Spirit into our expressions of willpower.

The middle finger represents the concept of projection, which is different from affirmation. Projection is the expression in the outside world, of what we bare inside. This finger is associated with the element of fire, the element of force in action. In the left hand, it expresses the human means and actions. In the right hand, it is the movement of experiences and events.

The ring finger is the finger of sensibility and adaptation. It is associated with the element of water, flowing softly according to outside forces. In the left hand, it is feeling and permeability. In the right hand, it is awareness and resilience.

The pinky finger represents the concept of consolidation. It is associated with the element of earth, grounding its stable presence. In the left hand, it will be represent the understanding of knowledge and, astonishingly, grounding the human experience. In the right hand, it will represent the integration of the experience, the assimilation of wisdom.

It is not essential to remember all of these details when you read them at first. Each mudra of Kuji-In will be explained, and the interaction of each finger with the others will make more sense, helping you understand the symbolic nature of each mudra, rather than simply remember all of this by hearth.

Now, as for the way to cross and bind fingers, some traditions place the bent fingers inside the hand, and others keep the fingers outside the hands. For example, in the application of RIN in the Transformational Approach, the bent fingers are kept outside the hand, while in KYO, the bent fingers are kept inside.

RIN

KYO

Keeping bent fingers outside triggers a relationship with the outside world, or contributes to a manifestation, while keeping bent fingers inside the hand will focus on what is going on inside us, and contributes to our awakening. In our application of RIN, we wish to develop self-trust and faith, thus affirming and exteriorizing the experience of life symbolized by the extended middle finger. As for our application of KYO, we wish to become aware of our sense of responsibility, thus we keep the earth and water fingers inside the hand, while the air finger bends over the fire finger and returns to the void finger. A few variations will be presented in later pages.

From Sanskrit to Japanese, and back

The original Buddhist mantras used in Kuji-In were in Sanskrit. The mantras were thought orally for quite a while, until they were written down using the Sanskrit alphabet. At this point, nothing else would have been expected.

In time, Buddhism went from India to China and from China to Japan. Once in Japan, the Japanese Buddhists wrote the mantras using their own alphabet. The Japanese alphabet is composed of symbols that are called "kanji". Each kanji represent an idea, and is spoken by a simple syllable. But these kanji syllable do not cover all the possibilities of vowel and consonant combinations. For example, in Japanese, the letter R and the letter L are the same, and it is pronounced as a hybrid of the two, like quick R followed by a mute L. It could be written in English as "rL" but would not be clear enough for us. In the same manner, there is no B or V, but a crossing of both, like a percussive V, or a blown B.

When the Japanese Buddhists wanted to write the Sanskrit mantra "Om vajramaanatayaa swaha", they used the Japanese kanji that were closest to the Sanskrit pronunciation. To start with, the "Om" became "On", since the Japanese M and the N are the same. Then, the "Vajra" became "Bai Shira", crossing the B and the V, and crossing the J and the Sh. And so on. We ended up with the mantra "On bai shira man taya sowaka". After quite a while, the Japanese kanji were used "as is" for the mantras pronunciations. It did not mean that the mantras were lost, but a modification had occurred.

The most important part of Kuji-In is the contemplation of the philosophy behind the ritual practice. When mantras are used repeatedly according to a traditional use, the brain invokes an amount of energy corresponding to the implication of the practitioner in this tradition. Thus, all the monks, priests and martial artists that have been using the Japanese kanji did not lose their time. They simply used another set of beliefs to invest themselves in their personal development.

After centuries, the mantras were even slightly modified from one master to another, according to their own experience of Kuji-In. When they were translated back to Sanskrit, using only the study of corresponding pronunciation as a reference, they might have gone thru yet another level of modification. The beauty of it all is that the sense of the practice did not alter, and the Sanskrit mantras we use today are profoundly linked to the entire practice and philosophy of each of the Kuji-In.

The Japanese mantras tend to be used in martial arts and mind training, while Sanskrit mantras tend to be used in devotional and spiritual practices. The first mantras that are thought should be the Japanese kanji version. They are mentally as efficient, and trigger the same attributes from the brain when combined with the philosophical contemplation. Once a seeker has shown some level of interest in the practice, clearly leading beyond mere curiosity, the Sanskrit mantras can be revealed and explained without fear of lacking respect in the sacredness of these mantras. The personal growth involved in the advanced Kuji-In teachings is a great filter to block out the superficial student. The mind training can be enough for them; they have no use with the sacred wisdom.

Some say that the Sanskrit mantras are more powerful than the Japanese mantras. We could say that the Sanskrit mantras are usually reserved to those who have faith in a spiritual universal concept. Those who do not have such a faith should not bother with the Sanskrit mantras. If there are no greater universal force at all, be it God or another concept, then in an atheist's mind, only the psychosomatic effect of the mantras would count, thus the Japanese mantras are all indicated. Only those who thrive to develop a deep faith should bother with the Sanskrit mantras, since they are the mantras that open to the spiritual aspect of the Kuji-In practice. Starting with the Japanese kanji pronunciation is not a waste of time, but a good preparation. The Sanskrit mantras will add depth to the practice when they are learned. Nevertheless, without faith, the Sanskrit mantras are useless. Therefore we should keep these mantras sacred and deliver the mentally efficient Japanese kanji mantras to the general public.

Further in the book, each of the nine mantras will be written, using our alphabet, in the Japanese kanji pronunciation, followed by the Sanskrit pronunciation, followed by an attempt in English translation. Then, they will be explained with details about their relation with different applications, religions, and traditions.

Light and Diamonds

What is a Vajra

The light of creation, the original burst of willpower, emitted by the absolute Divine truth in a wish to discover life by observing itself in manifested existence, exploded into a creator's burst of pure light and sound to create the universe in all its various manifestations.

"Vajra" is a Sanskrit word that engulfs this concept. It represents all that comes out of the universal source in a pure state of light, sound, or vibration whatsoever. It is a concept hard to grasp and difficult to adapt to tangible concepts, so much signification it holds.

If the Vajra is followed by the Sanskrit syllable "man", it could mean that it is made to be more tangible. Thus, the Sanskrit word Vajraman commonly means "diamond" per se, as in "pure light made material". Yet, it does not necessarily mean "diamond" in every sentence. Sometimes, Vajraman could simply mean that the light of the Vajra is tangible, or manifested.

In Sanskrit, each work can hold many different significations depending on the context. Then again, maybe we are trying to put modern words over concepts that simply do not exist in our language, leading to the use of cross-concept words in Sanskrit.

When reading, and especially translating Sanskrit, every word and every sentence should be contemplated to find out the core concept that lead to its creation. This contemplative study usually helps our mind to let go of our traditional rigid definitions of the world, leaving much more room for our Spirit to inspire our mind.

Always bring back to your self.

Kuji-in was meant for the development of self. Thus, in every situation regarding your development of the technique, you should bring the philosophical concepts back to yourself. Before you project your energy outwards, you have to become aware of in inwardly.

When we will say, later on, that the word TOH is Japanese for "fighting", you will have to set your mind in a receptive way so that you can pay attention to the concept of fighting, rather than set yourself in a mood for fighting. You will be required to be stronger than any urge to fight what surrounds you, and you will have to be at peace, paying attention inside you, at what the concept of "fighting" awakens from within.

For every one of the following concepts, you will have to practice self-mastery, by discovering the essence of the feelings they stir up inside, and becoming aware of the emotional triggers attached to the concepts. Discover from within, what seems to be without, and you will know yourself more.

RIN

RIN Consciousness

In the introductory and advanced knowledge of the Kuji-In, we learned that RIN was implicated in the concept of trust. We first learned that we should work to become courageous. Courage eventually leads to trust, which leads to self-trust. In time, self-trust will lead to Faith in the self, and then in a universal spiritual concept such as God or the higher self.

Each time you succeed something, you should focus on appreciating this success. This will help you build foundations for your mind to believe you can be successful. In this way, you will gain self-trust thru perseverant application of mental training practices, but also thru life experiences. Yet, whenever you fail, or believe you failed something, you should spend more energy on fighting negativity, and keeping your morale up. Use your apparent failures to build your determination to succeed by refining your future attempts. Trust in your ability to become better.

RIN Technique

RIN mudra

The RIN hand seal binds all fingers together except for the middle fingers, which is the fingers of experiences and events. The middle finger extends to make contact with these experiences.

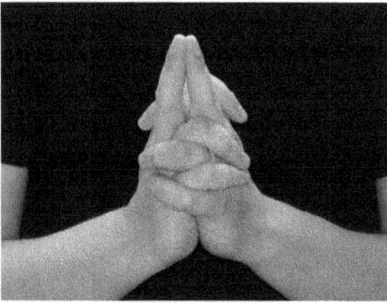

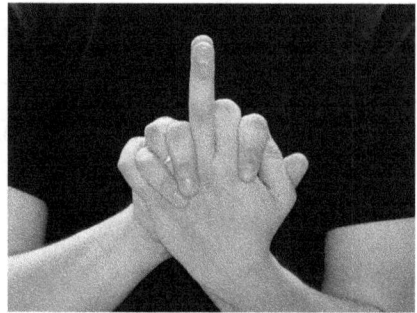

This mudra brings the human and spiritual hands together, so that the human and the spiritual self can join in life's experiences. This mudra helps to develop consciousness of each of the experiences that we are going thru, thus making them easier to accept and understand. This is the first step in becoming aware of the creative essence that leads to the manifestation of experiences and events in our lives. Knowing that there is a spiritual force creating all these experiences makes them easier to accept.

In the Transformational Approach, the RIN mudra keeps the bent fingers outside the hand, which means we are focusing on affirming our self-trust and faith. We seek to encourage it, and not only become aware of our actual level of faith.

Using this mudra will also help us trust that all will be fine. Accepting, even inviting our Spirit to accompany our human in its challenges, makes it all look like a lesson, rather than a punition. Whatever happens, if I believe that I am not alone, but steadily with myself as Sprit, it is obvious that everything will be fine, eventually. This is the faith of the Kuji-In, which has nothing to do with having faith in an exterior God. Faith is the ultimate self-trust as Sprit as well as human, as one. Breathe NOW.

Some Kuji-In traditions will express the index outward instead of the middle finger. Extending the index represents the affirmation of power, as a decree of the self. This version of the RIN mudra will be more frequently used by martial artists and people who wish to build a stronger willpower. The transformational approach encourages the experience (middle finger) of RIN at first, followed by the affirmation (index) of RIN only when much more experience has been gained. Experience and faith is essential to the true expression of power.

RIN mantra

Rin, in Japanese, means *face* or *meet*. It has to do with meeting someone, without indication to who we are to meet; thus, we meet ourselves. To meet your self implicates to get to know yourself by observing yourself in a "third person" perspective. Such contemplation, in an honest attitude of self-acceptance, will inevitably lead to trusting yourself.

Jap. Knj:	On	bai shira man	taya	sowaka
Sanskrit:	Om	vajraman(a)	taya	swaha
English:	O	thunderbolt	to / who has	glory
Pronounced:	Om vajramaanatayaa Swaha!			

Shinto: In this kuji-in practice, the Shinto Buddhists are referring to Amaterasu, a feminine Goddess. Amaterasu is described as the Goddess from which all light emanates, and is also often referred to as the sun goddess because of her warmth and compassion for the people who worshipped her; an interpretation of "light" or "heat" as passion, or purity. She emits lightning into the body to give it life force. She is like the light of creation.

Buddhists: Here the Buddhists pray Bishamonten, guardian of the north, and thus, of material things. From the traditional Japanese Buddhism point of view, since the time of samurais and great warriors, he is said to be the god of war and warriors. Bishamonten is wearing an armor symbolizing the physical shell over his true self. He holds a spear in one hand, a symbol of the Spirit that penetrates the physical world, and a pagoda in the other hand, like a temple where wisdom resides, another symbol of our physical body.

Hindu: Most of the Kuji-In process invokes the hindu God Indra, who is the only King of heavens, holding thunderbolts. The word swaha can be translated as glory, homage or salutations, but is used mostly when doing prosternations, offering sacrifices. Thus, this mantra is also a pledge of sacrifice offered to the God King of Heaven, Indra, know as the one who holds thunderbolts. The Hindu tend to interpret each word with all their possible meanings according to their religious structure, therefore a few Sanskrit words become much longer phrases so that they can transmit all the meaning at once. This Sanskrit mantra could mean, in Hindu terms: Om (Holy Word), I offer sacrifice by the name of the God, who carries Vajra in his hands i.e. Lord Indra.

Transformational approach: We contemplate the powerful force of creation. We contemplate the light that comes from the heavens down into the earth to give it life and movement. This Light is both feminine and masculine. At this point, we celebrate the coming of the Spirit into the human body.

In our tradition, Om vajramaanatayaa Swaha!
Means: O, Divine Light of Glory

Remember that it is also an interpreted translation, since the Sanskrit words are linked to many meanings and possible significations. Here, we have translated *vajraman* as Light made tangible. We use the sanskrit swaha to proclaim the glory of God (or universal concept of your choice), and to pay homage.

Life entering the body can be symbolized as a lighting bolt that strikes stone, like a heavenly spark kick-starting the mechanism of life in a physical host. On a softer tone, we could imagine a ray of light that heats up the earth and progressively make it to become alive. This birthing of the Spirit into the human body is of a feminine energy, like any kind of birthing. Yet, it is powerful enough to create movement where there was none. It doesn't have to be as violent as striking lightning, but the symbol is still as powerful as it was meant to be.

If we lookup a Sanskrit dictionary, *vajraman* will mean diamond, but we still have to analyze the particles one by one. The Sanskrit word *vajraman* is a symbol of the purest light of the *vajra*, made physical by the syllable *man*, thus it was the name applied to a diamond.

The *vajra* is this wonderful heavenly light that takes many shapes depending on the other terms that surrounds it. Followed by the syllable *man* to make it physical, and the word *taya* to make it feminine, it is the Heavenly Mother's light of creation. With this prayer, we invoke the light that made us to be alive, which is still and will remain the source of our human life. Do not imagine that a feminine light would mean it is weak. A mother giving birth is very powerful.

When we first entered life, as a Spirit into a human body, we became alive without any kind of judgment of ourselves, thus without fear, hesitation or doubt. Our progressive human conditioning, mostly thru unpleasant childhood experiences, brought us to be more than simply careful not to get hurt, but to fear and doubt ourselves. Now grownup, we believe we have conquered most of these fears, but it is not true. There are fears we would not even admit to ourselves so deep are their roots in our subconscious memories.

We are not only talking about those cases of difficult childhoods. Even in a happy childhood may a child bump his head and not like it, and react with anger against the pain or with guilt towards the lack of agility, blocking some part of the subconscious mind with self-hatred for not being perfectly stable already. There can be hundreds of reasons why we defined ourselves with poor self-trust even in our first life experiences. Now, you can imagine the results of a difficult childhood added to that.

The goal of the RIN technique is to redefine the concept of trust, and apply it to ourselves as self-trust, and from that, grow it to become faith in life. When the concept of faith is removed from the dogmatic teachings of religion, it is a higher form of self trust, knowing that from the point of view of the Spirit, everything will always be fine.

Although your human body can be injured, and your human experience can sometimes be painful, your Spirit is totally unaffected. Experiencing human existence as an observer as much as a participant, it remains beyond the reach of possible harm. RIN is the awakening of such spiritual memory, and it takes full reach as you progress towards the RETSU technique, where you may even remember the immortality and eternal existence of your

Spirit. At this point, everything you will experience will be seen in yet a much broader perspective.

KYO

KYO Consciousness

Being in charge of your life does not mean to be in control of your life. Control holds a sense of pressure over the events to prevent them from happening in ways other than how you had planned them. While true self-mastery involves letting go of control, and remaining in a state of faith towards life's events, while also consciously using all the tools that are available in order to influence the ways the events manifest to server one's goal.

Control is a state of mind where you mentally pressure yourself and others into a set of predefined expectations. Expectation will naturally lead to deception the moment control is lost. Control also involves fighting against all that would work in ways that differ from your expectations. This pressure and hassle consumes a lot of energy. Control is the opposite of letting go. Control is a temporary and hopeless way for the human ego to simulate a state of success. But control is costly in resources of all type, including life force and emotional stress. Thus, self-control, for example when you would find yourself in a state of anger, is a way to restrain yourself from giving in to the pressure that builds inside when you are emotionally unstable. It involves fighting against yourself and spending a lot of energy in a process that consist in holding back the animal human beast that only wants out. Self-control is not the same as self-mastery. Self-mastery would not even involve any inner pressure to fight with in the first place.

Mastery is a way to act from a point of view of consciousness. It is an awareness of the forces in operation, and an influence on their direction. Mastery is not fighting against a force, but an awareness of that force, triggering its unraveling, or calming it from within. Mastery relaxes a pressure rather than fight against it. Again, with our example of anger, mastery would start with a conscious contact with the emotional reaction, and work its way into relaxing it using tools such as compassion, tolerance and responsibility. A person in a state of self-mastery does not fight with an emotional pressure, but seamlessly releases it with awareness, using tools like forgiveness and emotional transmutation. The emotional energy thus becomes available again, regenerating the master instead of depleting his strength and life force.

Whenever a master faces a force that he does not understand, he must pay attention to it, contemplate it, taste it, discover all that he can about it, in a state of conscious contemplation, observing from both a human and a spiritual point of view. Mastery involves becoming aware of the forces in action, especially the forces from within the human nature. Only when the secrets of human nature will have been revealed to the pondering master, will the spiritual forces become clear and accessible enough to be grasped with the human mind. Until then, it is our responsibility to use the tools that are accessible to us in order to become aware of ourselves.

Responsibility starts when we understand the difference between control and mastery. To be responsible is to accept that we have the means to make our lives better, by making ourselves better in the first place. Being responsible is not only assuming the consequences of an event. Assuming a responsibility involves the understanding of the forces in action that lead to the events that manifested in our lives, so that we can become aware of how each specific event manifested as a result of natural and spiritual forces involved in a series of actions and reactions.

At the moment, such a concept seems very complicated, but it is so only because we are interpreting the concept of mastery with our human mind. The mind can only perceive parts of the equation at once, but consciousness always steps back to look at the full artwork, only to discover that the human mind was contemplating a limited square inch of a very beautiful wall painting. Consciousness does not require that all be interpreted intellectually. While we pay attention to ourselves and the forces within us, we become aware of the entire process at a glance, and all seems so simple. For example, it is not necessary for us to intellectually understand and control all the physiological processes going on in our body when we dance (blood pressure, nervous stimulation of the muscles, the mathematics of coordination, balance information coming from the inner ears,…). We only have to dance and the beauty of it is revealed.

Mastery is first attained by letting go of the limits we pose on our perception tools. It consists in accepting all the information that is revealed when we pay attention. Our awareness of ourselves grows and expands as we accept what we perceive of ourselves. From that point on, consciousness is naturally infused in the forces we became aware of, giving us the means to influence them.

Without extending ourselves on the subject, we can resume "Karma" as being a lesson that is manifested in your live so that you may learn about yourself through experience. Experiencing emotions and sensations of all sorts help you understand different lessons in life. Karma is not a consequence as much as a voluntary lesson from the point of view of the Spirit.

A consequence is the result of a previous action. It is often associated with guilt in the thinking process of "it happened because of me, thus I am guilty". Being responsible means that you will assume the consequences of an action, but it does not mean you are guilty. Guilt is the result of not accepting our moral responsibility, or subtly fighting against responsibility. Guilt happens out of self-judgment when we prefer not admitting the truth to ourselves about a certain situation.

Throw pebbles in the pond and look at the ripples behave. The pebbles do not experience guilt. They are responsible for the ripples, so is the water. If you study the natural phenomena of action and reaction, you will understand more the subtle concepts of responsibility.

Our human ego likes to pressure itself under the weight of guilt, by playing a game of victim, especially if this role serves the human ego to attract more attention to it. You will free yourself from the emotion of guild by admitting the truth to yourself out of a context of a victimizing game. Always take the time to breathe into your emotion; it will help you become aware of them.

To become the master of your life, you must let go of control by responsibly accepting whatever happens to you, while also taking command by acting in ways to produce the results you wish to manifest. Accept illness when it strikes, and do all you can to prevent it. Accept pain when there is pain, and do all you can to responsibly resolve the pain.

By subtly accepting that you are a part of all that you experience, and that everything manifests in your life in some way because you have desired it either from the human or spiritual point of view, you will also develop the power to manifest what you wish for by taking control of your desires. While you endure a painful human situation, even when you consciously do not desire this situation at all, there are unconscious mental processes that allow the painful experience to perpetuate itself. The more you become aware of your ego's self-defense mechanisms and hidden follies, the more you become the master of what you manifest.

From a point of view, your human ego does not mind you endure pain, if it serves it to attract attention and nourish the fantasy of its false life. From another point of view, your Spirit will respect your choice of lessons. Your Spirit does not see pain where you perceive pain; it only sees experience. It is You, in the middle of it all, that have to take command (again, without taking control) and become a master of what you manifest. In time, you will remember where you situate yourself in your own experience. You will remember that you are your human ego, that you are your Spirit, and that you may chose your point of view in every situation.

KYO Technique

KYO mudra

The KYO mudra pulls the middle fingers of experience in contact with the contemplative thumbs of consciousness, so that the experience may be perceived globally and integrated as consciousness of life experiences. The experience fingers then wrap around the indexes of affirmation, to enlighten and direct the affirmations with wisdom. Therefore, this mudra help you become aware of what you manifest when you affirm something, and it helps you become a master of your life by assisting your affirmations with the wisdom of integrated experiences.

In some traditions, especially because it is difficult to do so, the middle fingers don't bend enough to touch the tips of the thumbs. This is not dramatic, since it does assist the process of affirmation with the experience one has of life. Yet, when the mudra is done this way, it will not assist the seeker in gaining experience faster.

We keep the ring and little fingers inside the hand, meaning that we focus on becoming aware of the concepts of responsibility. We wish to develop a consciousness of being in charge, and for this awakening to happen we must be able to perceive these energies of action / reaction, of shock in return, from within us. In other traditions, keeping the last 2 fingers outside will work on expressing that you are in charge. Such a tool could be useful to impress people or defend yourself, but does not make you more responsible unless you learn from the inner contemplation of the concept.

From an elemental point of view, the experience of life previously extended in RIN, is now wrapped around the moving air, blowing towards our spiritual consciousness. The air/index emits an active energy, like an action, and the returning reaction is the fire/middle finger turning back to be absorbed in the thumb/spirit.

KYO mantra

Kyo or Pyo means *strategy* or *troops*. Observed outwardly, the concept of troops holds little sense in relation with the kuji-in practice. If we bring the concept inwardly, the strategy is what we must operate in order to manifest what we desire, and the troops are the means that are available to us. It refers to the organizing of our actions in order to attain the desired result.

On	isha	naya	in tara	ya	sowaka
Om	isha	naya	yantra	ya	swaha
O	vigorous	behavior	instrument	the one	glory

Pronounced: Om ishaanayaa yantrayaa Swaha!

The Shinto religion refers to Hachiman, a God of war, giving his grace of abundance to fishermen and farmers. Hachiman was a God of war at the time of the samurai, where it was necessary to fight and protect if one was to obtain and keep riches. But what would be then, his relationship with fishermen and farmers? Hachiman explains to us how to act in ways to attain what we seek by adequate and determined actions. While we do not need to physically fight anymore, Hachiman still is a model of determination and discipline.

Buddhists pray Juichimen, with a thousand arms and eleven heads. The eleven heads symbolize the many ways his power would manifest, and the thousand arms represent the many ways of actions taken to attain a goal. The statue of Juichimen at the Sanjusangen-do temple has 40 arms, and each are said to save 25 worlds, totaling 1000 worlds.

The Hindu might translate this mantra as: Om (Holy Word), I offer sacrifice by the name of God's weapons. They would reference the instrument as being a weapon.

In our tradition, Om ishaanayaa yantrayaa Swaha!
Means: O, Mastery for Instrument, Glory to the Divine

We consider our vigorous or rightful behavior to be self-mastery, which is the instrument we use to be responsible. We present our homage to the Divine, or God, allways present by the Om.

Practice this mantra while holing in mind that you are responsible for everything that ever happened to you, if only from the point of view of Spirit, manifesting the lessons and the trials, but also the blessings and good fortune. By acknowledging this creative phenomenon, and by freeing yourself from the emotion of guilt, you will start developing your power of manifestation. By perceiving the concept of manifestation from the point of view of the Spirit, you will allow your conscious mind to accept this power as a truth, thus, realizing it in your conscious human experience.

Give time to your human mind to change, to let it transmute into a tool of a higher level of consciousness. In time, with patience, faith in your spiritual self, and determination, you will allow greater levels of creative energies to enter your human life. When this energy enters your conscious mind, it will take the flavor and the taints of your thoughts. The creative energy of the Spirit will follow its course thru your body, emanating outwards into your life, so to manifest the events that correspond to your thoughts. Henceforth, if you ever have bad luck, question yourself as to if you had a clear mind lately. You might discover that you have even more responsibility in what you manifest than before. Even in unfortunate events, this creative process is a blessing, as it helps to condition your mind into accepting that you manifest from what you thought before.

Train your mind into being happy. Train your mind into being simple. Believe in good deeds and events. Have faith that everything will always be fine. Mostly, give yourself the time to attain this point of clarity and happiness. Do not discourage yourself, and trust yourself that everything will always be better.

TOH

TOH Consciousness

We all have a place inside where we fight against ourselves. We all have these resistances to change, these opinions we hold dearly, these protective reactions that we keep with all our willpower while we are convinced they are legitimate protections. Our human ego starts off any subject with the point of view that it holds the truth, and that it is the most important aspect of the equation of life. Thus, we fight to keep our fears, our guilt, our sadness inside of us, like treasures we cherish.

These are the fights we have with ourselves, and these fights are what consume the most of our life energy. We cannot resolve a conflict while we remain unaware of it. By becoming aware of the battles that rage within, we are allowing the release of all these tensions and energy blockages, making the entire process of living much easier. Once an inner battle is allowed to exist, it expresses itself and we can then take action in ways to transform the situation in something positive. Sometimes, the rage simply wished to be heard, and it will find peace with the satisfaction that it got the inner attention it desired. These inner battles originate within our human ego, and paying attention to them is often a great part of the solution. Yet, we will find it hard to pay attention to what we do not acknowledge within ourselves.

While a role of the ego is to attract attention to it, another one is to entertain its fantasy of itself. Thus, as a human ego, we lie to ourselves, not allowing the truth of what we feel to rise up to consciousness. This is the work that has to be done in the process of the TOH technique. It is a process of acknowledgement of the truth, followed by the letting go of the battles that rage inside us.

When we are done releasing the pressure of our most intimate inner battles, our entire energy system is freed and can function with much more efficiency. Do not fool yourself; kings, beggars and saints all have these inner battles going on, even at the most subtle level. We are free from inner fighting only when we have totally conquered our human ego.

TOH Technique

TOH mudra

The TOH mudra is the most passive and contemplative of all Kuji-In mudras. With the perceptive thumb of consciousness, the sensible ring finger and the stabilizing pinky finger, this mudra help us to perceive what is going on, while our affirming index and experimental middle finger are focusing inside. If there is affirmation, it is done inside. If a feeling is experienced, it is experienced inside.

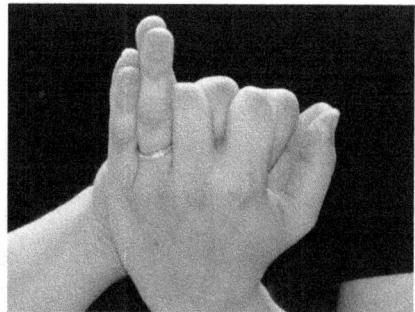

We keep our air and fire fingers inside, to become aware of the motion of energies triggered by the conscious, sensible and grounding fingers seeking harmony. Keeping index and middle fingers outside the hand would try to impose peace rather than become aware of it, yet it would still be a mudra of peace and harmony.

In some traditions, this mudra is called the outer lion, and many attempts have been made to explain why it would be named "outer" while it is aimed at inner peace. The reason for this is simple. This mudra is called the "outer lion" in its shape of the Shinto tradition, where the index and middle fingers are intertwined to express harmony by force, a typical trait of the martial arts mudras. When the TOH mudra is done in this manner, it looks like a lion going towards the outside, or perceived from other people's point of view. It is done by inserting the index fingers in the dent between the ring and middle finger, than bending the middle fingers over the indexes.

TOH mantra

Toh means *fighting*. Outward fighting is what we usually do when we are confronted with difficult situations. But if we take the concept of fighting inwardly, we discover the fighting we lead against ourselves, preventing us from attaining peace and harmony. This concept refers to the contacts we have with others, as well as with ourselves. In order to find peace, we must understand our own personal fights.

On	je te		ra shi	itara	ji ba	ra ta no-o	sowaka
Om	jita		rashi	yatra	jiva	ratna	swaha
O	conquering		zodiac	place	life	treasure	glory

Pronounced: Om Jitaraashi yatra jivaratna Swaha!

The Shinto god Kasuga, a deer deity, is a messenger between our human mind and our interior spiritual world. The zodiac being the influences over our character and personality, it is compared here to the lower influences over our life. Many different things influence our decisions and actions. These influences come from others and from our selves. Having conquered these subtle influences, we rejoice of our new life.

The Buddhists pray Nyorin Kannon, a bodhisattva that fulfils any wish and desire, making life so wonderful. He is pictured sitting at ease, meditating, and the innermost of his six arms is holding a jewel of happiness and wisdom that grants the wishes of the devoted prayer.

From both a Buddhist and Hindu point of view, the zodiac also represents what is keeping us in the cycle of reincarnation. The zodiac is the path that we travel with our human ego, to discover who we truly are, in every possible aspect. Once freed from our human ego's control, our perception changes and everything becomes marvelous and beautiful. The Hindu could translate this mantra as: Om (Holy Word), I offer sacrifice by the name of the various Rashis/Zodiac signs with their corresponding auspicious ratnas/stones etc.

In our tradition, Om Jitraashi yatra jivaratna Swaha!
Means: O, conquering the zodiac, journey to life's treasures, Glory

Pay attention to your inner fighting. Become aware of it to dissolve it with conscious acknowledgement of it. Breathe into it and relax it from the depths of your anger's origins. Yet, do not drop hope, faith and willpower in such a process. Keep your energy up. This animal rage, this anger, is a legitimate aspect of our human experience and it should not be judged. It should simply be released of our ego's control.

Practice yourself at having a "happy rage" by shouting a big "WWWRrRrrrraaaaaAAAAAAH!" while smiling. Discover the power within the human animal rage, in an attitude of attaining success, without the attitude of overpowering others. Bring this animal anger to yourself and profit from it. Do not project your animal anger to others, but use it to fuel yourself when you need willpower. From the point of view of the Spirit, anger and joy are the same energy with different polarities. Anger is a pressure that wants out, so is joy. Repressing one or the other will only hinder your ability to develop great willpower, while accepting to express both joy and anger will release the pressure of inner fighting.

Remember that each time you express anger in a state of battle, fighting, or conflict, you are actually losing in favor to your human ego. Yet, you should not pressure yourself in restraining this anger inside. Thus, you will know on what aspect of yourself you have to work on. Expressing your anger in another's face is a lack of self-mastery. You can keep the pressure in until you are alone to process it. But don't forget about it and leave the pressure in, or you'll have other issues out of that. Ah! So much to do! Yes, be patient, determined, and you will grow on the path progressively. Eventually, you will be at peace in every situation.

Human Emotions, Human Ego

The human ego tends to appreciate what he has built of himself over the years. When we start to tamper with our inner constructions, it happens that our ego will prefer the stability and comfort of what he already knows of himself, thus limiting the possibilities for expansion.

At this point, you probably understood the importance of the Emotional Transmutation technique explained in the "Advanced" book. It is critical to allow yourself to become aware of the emotional sources of every conflict that you hold inside. The challenge is also the become aware of your inner truth without letting yourself disturbed by your human ego, who will sometimes collaborate, sometimes fight against the process.

Combine your emotional transmutation with the recognition of the human ego in his manipulative behaviors. Pay attention to your natural defensive reactions when you try to prevent yourself from becoming aware of what you are, in truth. These behaviors will be hard to discern at first. As you gain more experience, you will become more agile and efficient in recognizing yourself, and accepting yourself as what you are.

SHA

SHA Consciousness

The more you gain self-mastery over your anger, the more power will be available to you when you need it. SHA is a place of power, more specifically, willpower. It is the expression of power at the level where your human self can experience it clearly.

From the solar plexus, your energy circulates, not only within your body, but also outwards. This is the place where the inner wheels turn, making the outer wheels turns as well. With SHA, the solar plexus operates the movements that you set forth. It can call forth a rectification or it can set in place for destruction. Whatever your bidding, it will be powerful. Hence, this is the place where you must be careful not to hurt yourself or others.

Nevertheless, you are not left without tools. With the knowledge and wisdom to apply emotional transmutation, and the will you have to recognize your human ego at work, you are encouraged to trust yourself and follow the path to the development of your own inner power. This being said, let us define the first illusion of power.

When we first approach the concept of power, our human ego jumps in the scene shouting "This is my area! I know how it works!"… and we usually agree. This is the first mistake we do. Each time we mention "power", we believe it is a form of force or tightening of the muscles, accompanied by the stimulation of hormonal emissions, to provide a feeling of being powerful. This is a mask that the human ego encourages, hoping to prove to you that you are powerful from the point of view of your human animal. In fact, this muscular and hormonal power is a show that animals put on to prove themselves amongst other lowly creatures of a pack. This natural behavior often leads to the subconscious tightening of the buttock, waist and abdominal muscles, restraining the free circulation of "true" power within you. To attain a state of power, we must first release this biological tension we associate with the concept of power. The key to freedom is simple, you might have guessed already: pay attention.

Pay attention to the biological, emotional and mental reactions that you have when you contemplate the concept of "power". Before you are to develop true power, you must become aware of these hindering reactive behaviors that are mostly automatic defense systems. These defensive systems were useful for a great while, but now represent an obstacle to our full development. By processing these reactions, we will get to know ourselves even better, and we will start to dispose of a greater source of power for all our future experiences. Right now, take a moment to contemplate this wisdom and apply the technique to yourself, so that you may become aware of how you react to power.

Once aware of the way your human self deals with power, mostly from the point of view of its own fantasy of personal power, you can go on to letting yourself go to the true power that resides within you, and every where around you. The first step will be to let go of power. Let yourself become aware of universal, spiritual and personal power as one single force, unified and free flowing. Try to feel it without effort. Effort at this point will only be the ego's attempt to gain back the attention.

Breathe and feel. Let yourself become imbued with a feeling of strength while all your muscles are relaxed. Let the power of the universe grab you, penetrate you, imbue your every pore. The Power of the universe is a power that we let flow thru us, as we become a part of it. You do not control power. You simply become one with it, in consciousness, and then influence it with your will, not with your arrogance.

It is a natural reflex of the human ego to constantly jump out of its box with silent affirmations like "I'm stronger than…" or "I am more powerful than...". Every time you notice a form of pretentious behavior, it is the arrogance of your human ego. Become aware this personality trait and relax it.

We do not control the power of the universe, the Spirit and the human. We simply ride it. Let yourself flow with the power of the universe, let yourself become aware of its existence in your body. Gain consciousness of the all encompassing energy that surrounds and penetrate all things, this life, this great force that move planets and sand grains. This is the energy that fuels starts and your body's cells, the power that travels like light or stops in perfect immobility, while remaining alive in a still movement of life. We do not have power, we do not hold it, or possess it. We become it.

SHA Technique

SHA mudra

In the SHA mudra, we extend the index as an affirmation of power, while we also extend the pinky finger, to bring this energy down into earth. Combines with the thumb, this mudra helps us become aware of power, both human and spiritual, in our perceptible world. Extending the thumb, index and little finger, we wish to bring to earth the affirmation of our sprit. We will remain contemplative of this concept so it can penetrate us, while we keep the ring and middle finger inside our hands.

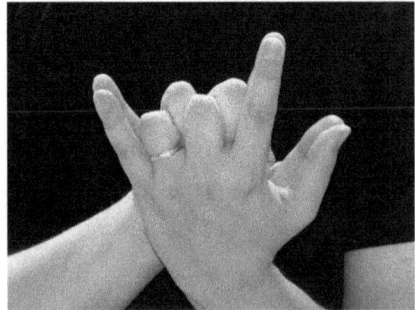

This mudra is also known as the inner lion, for the same reasons that the TOH mudra can be known as the outer lion. When you place the tip of your ring fingers in the dent between the middle and index fingers, then bending the middle fingers over the ring fingers, you end up having a lion facing inwards. If you orient the mudra upwards, and then look down over it, you will notice the thumbs and indexes making a mouth, the ring fingers making the eyes, and the little fingers making the ears. This mudra can be useful to force your sensible emotional side into affirming power. Again, while this application remains useful in conditioning yourself, it will not develop the actual awareness of your inner power as much.

SHA mantra

SHA means *person,* in Japanese. Obviously, if you follow the self-transformation way, this person is no other than yourself. With the Kanji RIN, you met yourself. Now, with SHA, you become this person that you met before. In fact, you allow yourself to remember that you are this self, from a spiritual point of view, yet affirmed in your human existence. Focusing on the concept of your identity, you affirm your right to live and act in power. In this action, power is revealed to your human self while you move into existence in the form of a spiritual living being.

Jap. Knj: On	haya		bai shira man	taya		sowaka
Sanskrit: Om	haya		vajraman	taya		swaha
English: O	ride	thunderbolt	to / who has		glory	

Pronounced: Om haya vajramaantayaa Swaha!

The Shinto refers to the God Kamo Daimyojin, a thunder God known to be a luxuriant being, usually celebrated with a horse race. The Buddhists will refer to Fudo Myo, the Immovable light, or Immovable wisdom, yet a symbol of power, since Fudo Myo is a powerful warrior.

In this mantra, the Sanskrit word *haya* is the English word *horse*, used in the sense of riding it. The SHA Sanskrit mantra is the same as the RIN mantra, with the exception that we are to ride the power, rather than invoke it.

We can see the close link between Amateratsu (Shinto goddess prayed in the RIN technique), the lightning Goddess, and the thunder God Kamo Dimyojin, but also with the Buddhist's Fudo Myo, the Lord of Immovable Light. Immovable, yet we invoke him riding a horse, which suggests interior immovability seated in free flowing exterior mobility. All these Gods and Lords are representation of the great power of the universe that condenses and flows through our human experience so that we may remember that we are one with this power. It is not required to use force to feel this ultimate strength, but simply to permit ourselves to vibrate it consciously. It does stimulate a feeling of power, yet not from the point of view of the human ego. If you contract your muscles too much while feeling this power penetrate you, then you are not letting go enough.

In our tradition, Om haya vajramaantayaa Swaha!
Means: O, Riding the Divine Thunderbolt, Glory

This mantra is spoken in an attitude of letting got, yet of encouraging the feeling of power from within. While we relax our every muscle, we focus on a peaceful yet powerful whirling power. It is not only a stream. It is everywhere, in movement. This force would seem to take us by force if it was not that we allow it to grab us fro within and flow thru us. We ride the power of the universe, and we influence it with our thoughts and our will. The "Glory" mentioned here is used to point out the glorious light creation, not to nourish an egotistical feeling of glory.

While in this process, do not actually try to operate a specific form of manifestation. Let yourself develop a relationship with this universal force. Later on, we will learn more about the power of manifestation, but for now, we must concentrate at developing the tools that we will use to influence the process of manifestation, eventually to provoke it. Until then, let yourself bathe in this happy turmoil of energetic life.

Healing and Rectification

From the point of view of the Spirit, there is only perfection in the experience of life. This perfection flows down into the human one plane of existence after the other. The light of perfection flows down into the soul, then the multiple levels of consciousness, the mind, the emotional body, the ethereal or willpower body, then into the physical body. When the light passed thru our human mind, it is tainted with the thoughts we have. When it goes thru our emotional body, it is tainted with our emotions. Same for the willpower body, it will be weaker if we are lazy or afraid; if we lack willpower. The light then becomes manifest in our body, taking the shape we have given it when it flowed down into our perceptible reality. For this perfect light of creation to flow freely from the Spirit to the human body, every plane of existence must allow its passage. The cleaner and clearer the passage from Spirit to body, the quicker the manifestation of the thought and emotions will be. This process is the major cause of our bad luck, and the reason why we are so much responsible for what we manifest, whether we are aware of it or not; whether we like it or not. Our mental and emotional attitude is more and more crucial as we develop our power of manifestation, since it will manifest in our lives what we think and feel.

Yet, this wonderful blessed mechanism of manifestation is also the process thru which we can heal ourselves, and eventually others. By rectifying our attitude towards life, by making our mind oriented positively, and our emotions free of pressure and judgment, we become available to manifest what we consciously desire. By mentally visualizing, emotionally desiring, and amplifying with willpower, we gain the ability to manifest.

The practice of SHA progressively develops our ability to flow with this wonderful creative light. It releases our ego's desire to control everything, leaving more space for us to commune with the light of creation, and to participate in conscious manifestation. The first manifestation of developing SHA will be the rectification of our body. This process will be progressive and can take quite a while to become apparent. It is not immediately miraculous-like. It can take quite a few years to accelerate the natural healing process up to a point where we can actually call it "regeneration". However, right from the start, it will make every healing process faster. It is a natural rectification of the human self operated by the Spirit into our manifested experience.

This process of rectification is not yet the full power of manifestation, but it is the preparation for such a power to take place consciously. It is from the point of view of the Spirit that we create. From the point of view of the human, we can only transform. Yet, this transformation can become quite efficient, since all that is done with the Spirit is done with great power and efficiency.

We do have karmas or lessons; judgments we hold tight to. These hinder the processes of rectification and manifestation. While we remain unaware or willingly unconscious of these inner battles, they sporadically manifest in the form of events, hopefully to trigger the expansion of our consciousness so that we may release the judgment we hold, and learn the lesson. These lessons will manifest at many level of experience, in the form of physical harm, emotional troubles or mental illness. As we become aware of these judgments, we can start selecting at which level of experience we prefer to assume these karmic lessons. Thus, when our body becomes sick, we can refuse the lesson and fight against it, or we can thank the body to assume this disease, so that other troubling events may not manifest in other ways. As long as the body can heal itself, some prefer to be sick rather than to have a bigger accident, or to face other life challenges.

This being said, the quicker you will acknowledge the truth behind the manifestation of your lessons, the faster you will heal or rectify the situation. The goal is still to become a master of your life and remove the victim stance your human ego so desires to keep.

Emotional pain, wounds and illnesses remain the manifestation of a poor mental attitude or emotional flaw or weakness of our will to live. The more you will amplify the flow of creative light from the Spirit to your human experience, the more these flaws will manifest, in the all-expansive goal to make your life better, by relieving you of your karmic weight. If you start using tools of power but don't clean up yourself as your consciousness expands, you will simply manifest more and more lessons to clean up until you are buried under them. At which point the Spirit will be clogged again behind the clouds of your hellish existence and wait for you to awaken again. Yuck! This is not welcome in the attitude of any spiritual seeker. Keep a positive attitude, and use the tools you have to make your life better, by becoming responsible of what you manifest and using your new power to rectify yourself where you need to. If we were to reveal the most powerful techniques to the new seeker, without giving them the tools to process their emotions and recognize their human ego at work, we would simply contribute to the destruction of their life. This is the main reason why the spiritual concepts thought in Kuji-In are to be instructed progressively in a wait to permit the student to absorb them each at their own rhythm.

The more you work on yourself, the more your healing power will develop, for you and others. While you cannot force this kind of personal growth on other, you can use it on yourself. The more enlighten you become, the more you will be able to shed this healing light around you, either willingly directing it, or nourishing it as a natural aura of healing around you. It is not yours to decide when other people face their demons. Do not burden others with personal growth if they don't wish it. Your healing assistance will help them at the level at which they are ready to receive it. It is for you to face your own demons so you can become a greater healer. Although some kind of personal growth will be beneficial in any healing process, others mostly need your compassionate love.

In the advanced book, the application of healing was explained. Do not hesitate to revise this information so that you can gain a better understanding of the visualization to hold in mind while you focus your attention on a healing process. Remember that the practice of SHA is not meant to heal, but to develop the healing ability. Once the healing ability is developed enough, you can use it to assist in the natural healing process of wounds and ailments.

KAI

KAI Consciousness

Unconditional Love comes as a result of unifying our consciousness with everything, created or not. The moment we encourage difference; we are not allowing ourselves to be unconditional. Yet, it is necessary to make differences, out of wise discernment, to manifest and experience a wonderful human life. As you accept in your human conception of life, that everything is bind from a spiritual point of view, your consciousness of everything will develop, and this will become perceptible in the form of a heightened intuition.

At this point, we will study the Tao of Kindness. In kindness, like in everything else, there is a light side and a dark side. Who would have guessed there is a bad side to kindness? Some may start to think about its different harmful manifestations, like when one is too kind and gives away everything even when hindering himself. But this is not the actual source of the dark kindness, only a result of it. The Tao of Kindness does not refer to the perceptible manifestations kindness, but to the original intentions behind it.

Most kind people develop kindness out of a desire to be loved, rather than from a desire to love. The kindness in itself remains a blessing and its manifestations are usually beneficial. Yet, what happens when someone is afraid to be pushed away then suddenly discover he is powerful and filled with self-trust? If the feeling of self-trust and power overwhelms such a person, maybe their might be no more motivations to remain so kind.

This process actually happens to absolutely all of us, without exception. Until we discover the beauty of kindness out of a desire to love others, the only motivation we have to be kind is from a point of view of a lack of love, thus our kindness disappears the moment we start trusting ourselves. We must not judge the kindness since it is a blessed action, whatever the intention motivating it. We must not speak of such a process to those who did not discover their own self-trust, as it would simply weaken their kindness. We simply must be aware of such a Tao, and recognize ourselves when we become subject to these changes of behavior. It is important to need to be loved. It is important to feel loved by others as long as we are in this state of experience. This need to be love will not go away until we attain a great level of enlightenment, thus it must not be judged. We are encouraged to accept ourselves at the level of evolution we are, and to progress in ways to become better persons.

Knowing about the Tao of Kindness is never a reason to underestimate kindness or to depreciate it. You simply must remain humble enough to recognize yourself each time a new aspect of you does not feel the need for kindness anymore, so you can replace the obsolete motivation for one of a higher level, which would be the desire to love unconditionally.

Kindness, whatever its motivation, out of love or lack of love, will never be a good reason to deprive yourself of your own integrity. Kindness is not a tool of self-destruction. It must remain free; free of charge and free of bounds. Kindness beyond self-preservation is only done out of a lack of self-love. From another point of view, kindness is not kindness if it requires an exchange. Although the exchange of kindness is always welcome in return, the requirement of an exchange for kindness to take place simply is not a true expression of kindness. Kindness is not a negotiation, and is not negotiable.

You do not have to be kind if you do not wish to. You must respect yourself in this. In time, you will be faced with life challenges that will teach you the importance of kindness out of your own good will. Kindness must not be forced upon your natural behavior.

Give yourself all the time you wish to notice how dark your life can become without free kindness as a loving tool.

Kindness is a blessing and it is the expression of love in our interactions with fellow humans. It is encouraged regardless of its motivations. Become aware of yourself in truth, and your intentions will become pure. Kindness in itself is always pure.

KAI Technique

KAI mudra

The KAI mudra is clear. We wish to bind everything together. And binding all of our fingers together will assist our mind in building new associations to comprehend that all in the universe is one. This concept of oneness will help us develop compassion and unconditional love, accepting everything as they are, making no more difference from the point of view of the Spirit.

Our application of the KAI mudra binds all fingers together in unification, balanced between the inside and the outside, between the completely exteriorized version made by keeping all fingers bent over the opposing hands, and the JIN mudra that keeps all fingers inside. Keeping all fingers intertwined together like this will make a mudra of unification of all things while clamping our palms together and having the fingers bend over the opposing hand will express compassion outwardly, which is also very good.

KAI mantra

KAI means *all* or *everything*. In this technique, you let yourself absorb by the grandiose concept of absolutely everything. Let your hearth feel love for everything without limitations and beliefs.

On	no-o maku	san man da	ba za ra dan	kan
Om	namah	samanta	vajranam	hâm
O	homage	everything	diamond	hâm

Pronounced: Om namah samanta vajranam ham!

The Shinto will refer to Inari, either and both a God and a Goddess of abundance. This availability to both sexes helps us detach the concept of love from sexuality, and teach us to love from the hearth regardless of sexuality. While sexuality is of great importance in our human experience, we have to train the human hearth to love regardless of the concept of sexuality.

The Buddhists will refer here to Aizen Myo, the Light of Passion where we see again a link to the hearth and feelings. The Light of Passion is not the dense passion we are used to at the human level. It is the Passion that the Spirit experiences towards all things. It's only possible manifestation of a great love for everything.

The Hindi could translate this mantra as: Om (Holy Word), I salute to his greatness, Lord Indra, who carries Vajra in his hands and also to all his ministers. They would refer to all the holders of the thunderbolt of Indra, instead of using the word "all" to point out everything there is.

We will remember that the Sanskrit word "vajraman" is the common word for diamond, but also an expression for the manifested or tangible luminous creative light. Here, "vajranam" is a more subtle light.

In our tradition, the mantra: Om namah Samantha vajranam hâm
Means: O, Homage to the Universal Vajra *Hâm*

The syllable Hâm remains a seed mantra that express the process of creation, thus it is not translated. It is not a word, but a tool.

Kuji-In Meditation

Set yourself in a meditative posture. Relax, clear your mind. Use your knowledge of Kuji-In to apply a quick focus ritual. Use each of the nine sets in nine breaths, saying the Sanskrit of Kanji mantras 3 times per exhalation. Visualize freely. The goal is to clear your mind afterwards.

Contemplate yourself as a human body. Take a minute to observer your physical identity. Then clear your mind about it.

Contemplate yourself as a human self, in its wholeness. Then clear your mind about it.

Contemplate yourself as Spirit, and pay attention for a minute. Do not define yourself as Spirit, but let Spirit inform you of it. Even if you don't see, feel, understand a thing, let yourself go to this experience. Then, let yourself gaze into emptiness and meditate.

Release all kind of mental attention. Gaze without effort, gaze in nothing, simply keeping a background thought that you are gazing at Spirit. Remain in this state, without mantra of mental activity, for as long as you can.

JIN

JIN Consciousness

JIN is a place of knowledge and expression. It is a point of view from which we observe the universe and its workings. It binds every part of us with every part of everything else. It is a place where knowledge is beyond understanding, and understanding is made possible only with the experience of the truth.

Truth is not a mere observable fact, but a concept from which we were created. While we practice ourselves at remembering who we are in truth, we open the gates to the pure knowledge of the Spirit. This knowledge is revealed by Spirit and it is acquired by human means. With patience, revelations will occur once in a while, each time clearer and stronger. The more you experience revelation, the more time will span between each of these experiences, but each time will be much more powerful. There will come a time when you will spend much time in a process of revelation and new knowledge will become easy to grasp. But this knowledge is not often easy to put words on, and we should not permit our human ego to pretentiously affirm that he holds the knowledge to something. Revealed knowledge is more often personal than general, and it does not always apply to the experience of others. You must allow yourself to become sensible enough to recognize a revealed truth from a fantasized dream of the ego.

An interesting side-effect of the development of JIN is the sporadic apparition of telepathic communications. These communications are not phone-to-phone streams of clear understanding. It does not even use words. While we gain experience in having our mind allow a free flow of knowledge and concepts, we might get to grasp concepts that took birth in the mind of others. But something is important to remember here. If we are to judge the perceived concepts only the slightest, the telepathic communication will not be allowed to occur, because of the presence of the human ego in the process. Thus, hoping to develop focused telepathic communication in order to find out information about certain facts, will simply give no handy results. Although you can practice at focusing your telepathic listening, mind reading depletes a great deal of energy when done from the point of view of the human ego, and you never have any guaranties that the information was not distorted by the same egotistical flaws to lead to such an outrageous misuse of this wonderful ability. It is recommended to simply let go of such ability and let it work its wonders by itself when we hold our mind and hearth in a state of humility and compassion.

JIN Technique

JIN mudra

While the JIN mudra does have an obvious similarity to the KAI mudra, the fingers connect to themselves from the inside of the hands, each tip touching the tip of the corresponding finger in the other hand. This mudra helps us get in contact with all the inner connections we make, at the level of the mind, the hearth, but also the Spirit. This is the mudra that gets every level in touch with the others so that a global understanding of every situation can be attained. JIN is affects both understanding and expression of knowledge. These inner bonds will eventually lead to the experience of knowledge without words. The deepest knowledge is made out of conceptual thought, un-worded and un-labeled by our human interpret.

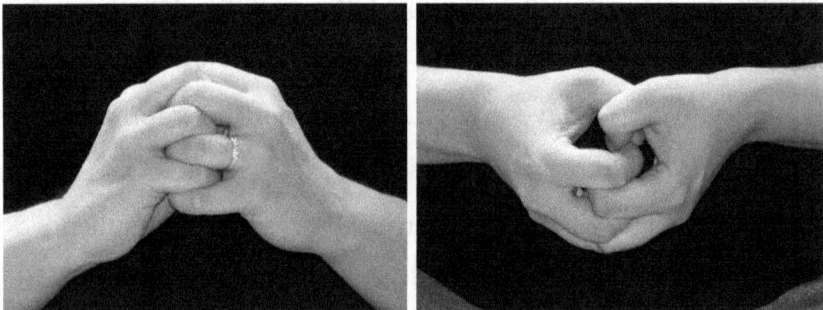

This mudra keeps all fingers inside, making connections from within, thus the development of understanding all things. This JIN mudra is the mudras that most of traditions use.

JIN mantra

JIN means *explain* or *demonstrate*. This kuji-in technique is the place of knowledge and understanding. It is where we learn by explaining to ourselves from Spirit to human, thus, knowledge gained thru inner observation and contemplation.

On	aganaya	in	maya	sowaka
Om	agnaya	yan	maya	swaha
O	fire of Agni	made of	surnatural	glory

Pronounced: Om agnaya yanmaya Swaha!

The Shinto prays Sumiyoshi, a god known for his love of poetry and the process of purification. The Buddhist prays Sho Kanzeon, which is another name for Avalokitesvara, the Buddha of Compassion. For the Hindu, it is a prayer to sacrifice our own negative thoughts into the fire of Agni.

The more we will advance in the spirituality of Kuji-In, the more abstract it will becomes. As we progress on the path to enlightenment, everything becomes clearer, yet the highest level of information comes from beyond the human mind. Thus, this elevated knowledge can take place in our human mind only thru the process of revelation, and the standard intellectualism becomes almost obsolete.

In order to perceive the highest knowledge, our mind must discover stillness, thru perseverant practice. When human joins Spirit in one single existence, the revelation occurs and knowledge from the universe becomes available to the human mind in function to its availability for this higher knowledge. Spirit never fights against the desires of the human, even the buried desires of ignorance. We are here faced to another challenge of befriending our human ego. Revelation can occur only when we admit we do not know. Yet, the reveled knowledge will tend to follow the subject we gaze upon. Thus, a lot of practice is required to develop a humble attitude, presenting to Spirit the knowledge we have as a human, and allowing to be enriched or rectified by the intervention of Spirit thru the process of revelation. We must willingly give permission to our Spirit to transmute us, even at the level of the mind.

In our tradition, Om agnayaa yanmayaa Swaha!
Means: O, Divine Fire which is Supernatural, Glory

It is a mantra of transcendence and transmutation. It is a calling to both human and Spirit to intervene in our existence. It calls for the stillness of our human so that Spirit can penetrate it, and in the calm of a heavenly bliss, we awaken to the supernatural truth about ourselves.

Revelation

In the next chapters, information will be given so you can contemplate it and allow yourself to learn from your Spirit. The true knowledge will come from progressive revelation, and this knowledge will be less likely to be transmitted to fellow humans, for it requires the availability developed over the years with the regular practice of Kuji-In.

Take the time to develop your abilities. Practice as often as you can. Do not trouble yourself with questions when you are concerned with the mysteries of Spirit. Do not rely so much on the knowledge you can acquire with human means, since this is now the field of the Spirit, and new knowledge in these areas can only be acquired by spiritual means.

Patience and determination will lead to success. Humility will lead to greater knowledge of the workings of the universe. Spirit is beyond words. Thus, revelation will take place without words, and you will get to touch the truth.

Retsu

Retsu Consciousness

We now stand in a transit area between dimensions. Space and time are only definitions that we placed over the mask of our own perception. From Spirit to human, and human to Spirit, there is no label, name, difference, or anything else that could be defined in ways to separate in levels or compartments. Yet, when our mind becomes aware of such dimensions, we naturally place images, sounds and feelings over the experience so we can integrate this new information in our human mind. This is a good way of interpreting the mechanisms of the universe, as long as we remember our thoughts remain interpretations. Each interpretation may differ from one's experience to another's, yet there are always similarities since it is the same universe observed from different point of views, in different ways.

RETSU is where we transmute the limits of perception. It is where long hour stop being tiring, and too short moments do not seem so fragile anymore. It is from this point of view where you may eventually remember the immortality and eternity of yourself as Spirit. Henceforth, human time becomes of a lesser importance in itself, but you must still remember your responsibility towards your human schedule. The same changes occur with your perception of space. Too small or too big are concepts that disappear, leading to the appreciation of whatever the size. From the moment you remember your wholeness as Spirit, the eternity and the size of your existence, every human measure loses gravity.

This new perception is a tool of great power for it releases the hold the human ego has over your perception. Yet, it is the place where spiritual ego takes every opportunity to lessen the value of your human experience. Yes, we could say we have a spiritual ego. In fact, human and spiritual egos are simply the ego seen from a different point of view. Nevertheless, the ego is present and he tries to limit the expansion of your consciousness. And he quite knows that you will expand your consciousness thru your human experience.

Remain responsible of your human measures, without allowing them to limit your experience of life. You will remember who you are once you become, as Spirit, fully incarnated in your human temple.

Retsu Technique

Retsu mudra

In this mudra, the index of the human hand thrusts its affirmation of life to climb into the channel of the Spirit hand, to finally get in contact with the spiritual expression and consciousness, the spiritual index and thumb. For some, it is a reference to the rising of the kundalini, which is the power of life that resides in the base chakra, and climbs up the spine once awakened. For others, it is the elevation of the mind to commune with the higher self. We could think it represents the human that crosses all the spiritual dimensions to attain enlightenment. I like to believe it is all of those interpretations and more.

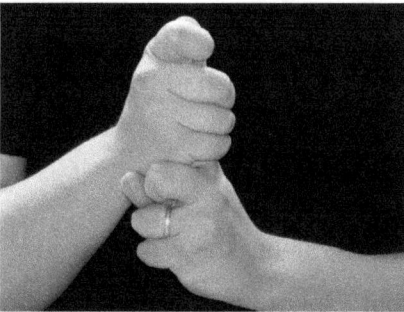

From an elemental point of view, the human mind, represented by the air/index finger of the left hand, is wrapped in every dimension of the Spirit, and commune with the spiritual void and air element.

Retsu mantra

Retsu means *split*. The first thing that could be perceived as splitting up, in creation, is the apparition of the concept of dimensions. Retsu corresponds to the multi-dimension universe we live in. This technique is a link between these dimensions, and it can be used to go up and to bind them, establishing relationships with many dimensions at the same time.

On	I ro ta	ki	cha no ga	ji ba	tai	sowaka
Om	jyota	hi	chandoga	jiva	tay	swaha
O	lighting /brilliance	for	chanting	life	stream glory	

Pronounced: Om jyota-hi chandoga jiva tay Swaha!

Note the pronounciation change of *jyota* to *jyoti* when linked to *hi*. This is one of the complexe aspects of Sanskrit.

The Shinto prays Nifu Daimyojin, known as the deity of Red Life. They refer to the red energy of life that cannot be extinguished and that keeps us alive longer. The Buddhists prays Amida Nyorai, or Amithabha Buddha, the Light and Long Life, again in reference to the eternity of our existence, or the extending of our lifespan.

The chanting mentioned here is a way to describe the vibration of sound. The light that we invoke here is the light that will help our life stream vibrate stronger. Our life stream is what links our Spirit to our human incarnation. It is the flow of divine light that traverses all dimensions and levels of experience from Spirit to human body. Thus, with this mantra we invoke the Divine Light that makes our life stream vibrate.

In our tradition: Om jyotihi chandoga jiva tay Swaha!
Means: O, Light that makes our Life Stream Vibrate, Glory

ZAI

ZAI Consciousness

We are the creators of whatever we experience. We are the masters of our lives. When Spirit comes from the heavens and descends into the human realms, we taint the light of Creation with the spoils or blessings of our human conditions, leading to the manifestation of everything we ever experienced.

At every level, purify yourself, transmute yourself, rectify yourself to become a pure temple of light and power. As you progress on the path, keep your focus on what is simple, happy and wonderful of your human experience, so to encourage it and progressively release you from the jail of judgment and sorrow. Keep a simple smile in your face. Be happy of your life. Do all that is in your power to make your life beautiful. It is your responsibility, and you have the tools to remain in the faith that you will succeed.

If there is every something specific you desire, be careful how you will enunciate your desire. Let's say, for example, you are wounded and you wish to heal. If your mental focus is "I heal my wounds", you will manifest tons of wounds so you can heal them.

If you wish to have enough money to pay your bills and focus on "I pay all my bills", you will create yourself so much more bills, so you can get to pay them.

When you wish to heal, focus on "I am healed" and visualize yourself healthy. When you wish to have lots of money, focus on "I have lots of money", and do not judge your focus. Often, the prime obstacle to a manifestation is the judgment we press against our element of focus. If you always say that money is dirty and used to create war, you will be less likely to manifest money, since you also desire peace. Be certain that you get to love what you wish to manifest. Transform yourself and release all judgments you hold before you operate a conscious process of manifestation.

I will not give a precise ritual of manifestation for now. It is preferable that you improvise while keeping the basic rules in mind, rather than following a precise ritual of manifestation. Once everything is clear in your mind, and your focus affirmation brought back to its most simple expression, combine all the tools you learned so far, and call forth the manifestation. Stretch out both your hands up and invoke the presence of yourself as Spirit, to come into your human experience, while you lower both your hands to make the creative light flow into the earth, and into the world around you. Be creative, say words that are simple and powerful. Enunciate your desire aloud (if you can), feel your desire, visualize, create it, while connecting to the high realms of Divine Light, bringing it down into the created world.

Remember that ZAI itself is not a ritual of manifestation, but a technique to enhance your creative abilities. After a great while of practicing ZAI, your power of manifestation will become more obvious and efficient. But right after the first time, you could feel the power of creation flow thru you. It might take quite a while to manifest your desires, but it will manifest if you also work with your human tools to make your desires possible.

If you wish to manifest Love in your life, but you never take any steps to meet people, you might actually manifest great Love from yourself to yourself. If you want a mate, go out there and find one, assisted by sporadic applications of your ritual of manifestation. Then, you must not judge what life will bring to you, but accept it as a new lesson.

Zai Technique

ZAI mudra

This is the mudra of creation and creativity. The indexes of affimation and thumbs of consciousness join together in concert while every other level of our experience, sensibility and

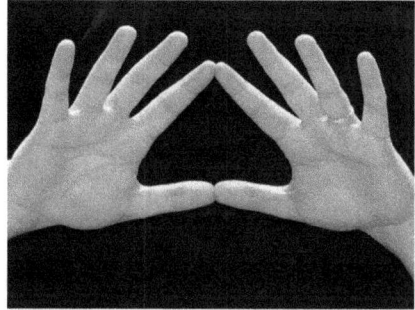

grounding is extended in every dimension, in ways to manifest the creative light that comes from the spiritual world.

In some traditions, the mudra is done by making a cirlcle with the indexes and thumbs symbolizing the sun, creator of all things. In other traditions the indexes and thumbs make a triangle pointing upwards, representing the elevation of the meditating mind. In each case, every other finger are extended to represent the phenomena of manifestation at every level. It is the air/index and the void/thumb that provoke the manifestation, and the fire/middle, water/ring and earth/pinky fingre that work the energies from there, operating the manifestation.

ZAI mantra

ZAI means *to exist* or *located somewhere*. It sometimes indicates a concept that resembles *something in the outside realms*. From the point of view of Spirit, existing outside refers to the concept of manifestation into dimension, thus, the phenomena of creation.

On	chi ri chi	I ba	ro to ya	sowaka
Om	sRj(a)	iva	Rtaya	swaha
O	creating	In a manner	the proper way	glory

Pronounced: Om srija iva Rtaya Swaha!

Here, the Shinto prays the sun deity Nitten Shi. The sun is the symbol of creation in many traditions. The Buddhist will pray Miroku Mosatsu, or Maitreya Buddha, who is the Buddha of the Future. As in future, we point out here to the concept of what will be, or what will become, referring again to the creation to come.

In our tradition: Om srija iva Rityaa Swaha!
Means: O, Creating with Perfection, Glory

Practicing this Kuji-In set will enhance your ability to create, which is your availability to let Spirit model your human experience in function of what you hold in your human focus, in your mind and your hearth.

ZEN

ZEN Consciousness

Human and Spirit always touch. In fact, they are the same thing, perceived from different points of view. Everything that you are, in every aspect, is but one single being, evolving thru many simultaneous dimensions and experiences.

Your body, your Spirit, and your hearth, are but one pure being vibrating in many frequencies at the same time, but never separated by any dimension whatsoever. Dimensions are but ways our human mind uses to label different levels of perception, multiple points of view. Nothing separates us in any way. We are whole, complete and perfect. Al that is left is for us to remember such a truth.

Kuji-In, in the transformational approach, will assist you in your evolution, from the resolution of your conflicts to the elevation of perception. It will help you release your fears, doubts, shame and anger. It will help you remember who you are, and to bring this memory back to light, in a conscious knowledge that you are one with yourself.

ZEN technique

ZEN mudra

In this mudra, the human completely relents itself to Spirit. The only aspect that remains active in the human hand is the thumb of consciousness, so that it can touch the consciousness of the Spirit. Other than that, the left hand lies over the bed laid by the Spirit. The Spirit hand receives the resting human hand, to care for it. This is the mudra know as the Golden Seal, in some Chinese Buddhist traditions.

Some traditions will place the fingers of the right hand in front of the left hand, cloaking it, and the left index also touches the tip of the right thumb. This mudra variation is mostly used in martial arts when invoking Marishi-Ten to shield us or hide us from enemies. Here are a few other known variations of the ZEN mudra.

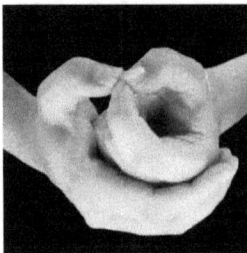

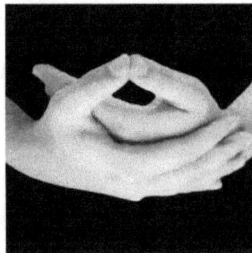

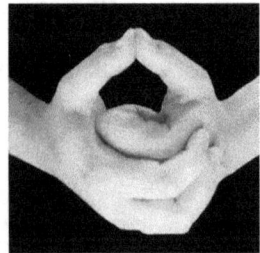

ZEN mantra

ZEN means *in front*, or *before*, in reference to the concept of obviousness. It takes a calm mind to perceive the most obvious essence of reality in a world filled with fantasy, dreams and fears.

Jap. Knj:	On	a	ra	ba	sha	no-o	sowaka
Sanskrit:	Om	ah	ra	pa	ca	na	dhi

As it is without translation in any language, this mantra is associated to what the Buddhists call the Manjusri Bodhisatwa mantra, also known as the invocation of perfection. The "ca" is pronounced "tcha / tsha" with an almost silent "t".

Said to cloak, even to render invisible, the Shinto prays the deity Marishi-Ten, the guardian of warriors. The Buddhist will pray Monju Bosatsu or Manjushri Bodhisattva, the Buddha of Wisdom.

In fact, it is the cloak of illusion that hides the truth that is taken away, while we use the invocation of perfection, at a point where our human eyes are allowed to shut enough for our spiritual eyes to perceive reality as it is.

This phenomenon greatly increases our vibration rate, which then makes it more difficult for other active human minds to accept the existence of such a heavenly presence in this world. Thus, without having us actually disappear, it might happen that someone does not notice your presence even while you should be apparent to them.

This mantra cannot have any meaning, thus we did not invent one for our tradition. We teach that this mantra is not meant to be understood, but simply to be uttered consciously, so to awaken the presence of the Spirit in our human world.

Meditate a lot, all you can. Take your time to forget your human self, so that you can get to know your spiritual self. Let the revelation of truth occur, and never be so impatient to share your findings with others, that will not understand the slightest of what you are saying. This technique is for you to use and discover. This is where the real path begins.

Conclusion

Where the path begins

This is where the true path of the master begins. This is where the application takes place. Henceforth, you have the tools to discover the profound wisdom hidden in but a few seals, words and images. You will become a master of this technique when you have let yourself touch by your Spirit.

Until then, you still are receiving the treasures of your practice. You learned (RIN) to trust yourself, even have faith in yourself, since (KYO) you are responsible (TOH) of harmoniously (SHA) harnessing the power, (KAI) elevated in compassion (JIN) for your greater understanding, (RETSU) so that by merging with your Spirit, (ZAI) you can create for yourself (ZEN) a life of perfection.

May you find yourself in truth, as Spirit. May you realize your full potential. May you remember who you are, delivered from all illusion. May you find peace.

MahaVajra

The seeker of Kuji-in mastery might want to pursue his implication by teaching Kuji-In of the Transformational Approach to fellow seekers. Certification in Kuji-In of the Transformational Approach is available via the website www.Kujiin.com

www.ingramcontent.com/pod-product-compliance
Lightning Source LLC
Chambersburg PA
CBHW060055100426
42742CB00014B/2842